Christmas
POPULAR PIANO SONGS

for KIDS

TOP Classical Christmas Carols
of All Time for Beginners

Arranged by
Alicja Urbanowicz

Piano Tutorial: https://youtu.be/3jWOUhqx8xY

Copyright © 2021 by Alicja Urbanowicz
Cover art: istockphoto.com
All Righrs Reserved

Christmas
POPULAR PIANO SONGS

Arranged by
Alicja Urbanowicz

CONTENTS

TITLE	PAGE
Angels We Have Heard on High	36
Away in a Manger	30
Carol of the Bells	42
Deck the Halls	40
Ding Dong Merrily on High	24
God Rest You Merry Gentlemen	14
Hark! the Herald Angels Sing	28
Jingle Bells	6
Joy to the World	38
O Christmas Tree	18
O Come All Ye Faithful	26
O Holy Night	20
Silent Night	16
The First Noel	32
Up on the Housetop	34
We Wish You a Merry Christmas	4
What Child Is This	10

We Wish You a Merry Christmas

Words: Arthur Warrell, 1935
Music: Arthur Warrell, 1935

We Wish You a Merry Christmas

We wish you a Merry Christmas;
We wish you a Merry Christmas;
We wish you a Merry Christmas and a Happy New Year.
Good tidings we bring to you and your kin;
We wish you a Merry Christmas and a Happy New Year.

Oh, bring us a figgy pudding;
Oh, bring us a figgy pudding;
Oh, bring us a figgy pudding and a cup of good cheer.

We wish you a Merry Christmas;
We wish you a Merry Christmas;
We wish you a Merry Christmas and a Happy New Year.
Good tidings we bring to you and your kin;
We wish you a Merry Christmas and a Happy New Year.

We won't go until we get some;
We won't go until we get some;
We won't go until we get some, so bring some out here.

Jingle Bells

Words: James Lord Pierpont, ca. 1850
Music: James Lord Pierpont, ca. 1850

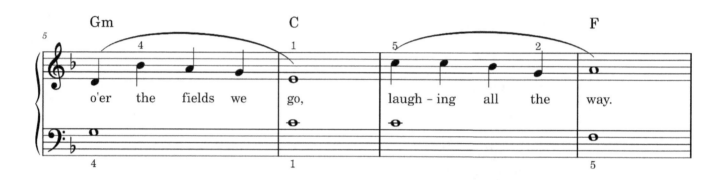
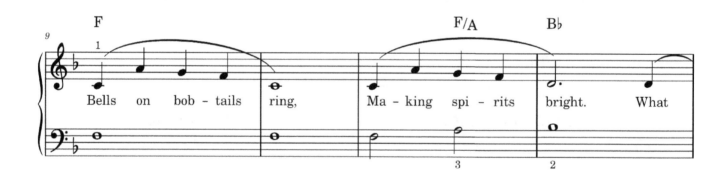
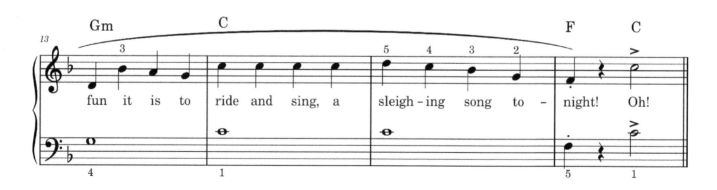

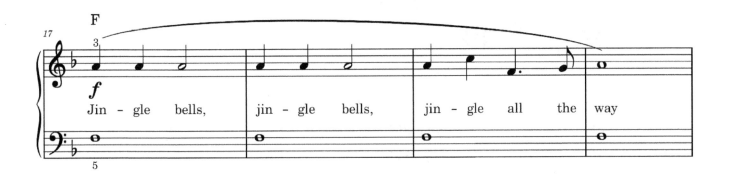
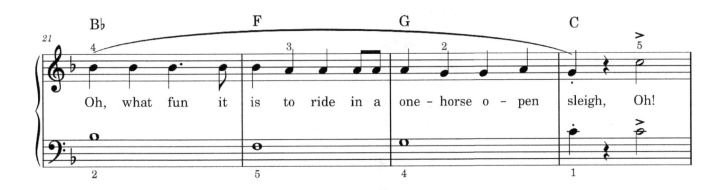

Jingle Bells

1. Dashing through the snow, In a one-horse open sleigh,
O'er the fields we go, Laughing all the way.
Bells on bobtails ring, Making spirits bright.
What fun it is to ride and sing, A sleighing song tonight!

> Jingle bells, jingle bells, Jingle all the way
> Oh, what fun it is to ride In a one-horse open sleigh, Oh!
> Jingle bells, jingle bells, Jingle all the way
> Oh, what fun it is to ride, In a one-horse open sleigh, Oh!

2. A day or two ago, I thought I'd take a ride
And soon, Miss Fanny Bright, Was seated by my side
The horse was lean and lank, Misfortune seemed his lot
He got into a drifted bank, And then we got upsot.

> Jingle bells, jingle bells...

3. A day or two ago, The story I must tell
I went out on the snow, And on my back I fell
A gent was riding by, In a one-horse open sleigh
He laughed as there I sprawling lie, But quickly drove away.

> Jingle bells, jingle bells...

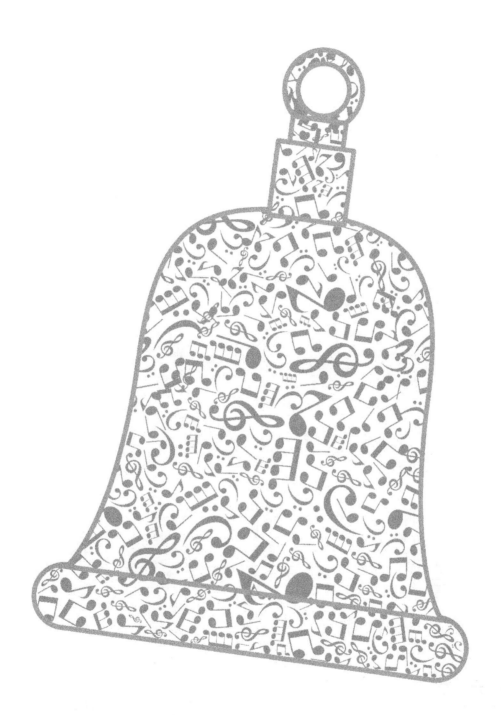

What Child Is This?

Words: William Chatterton Dix, ca. 1865
Music: Traditional English, tune of "Greensleeves"

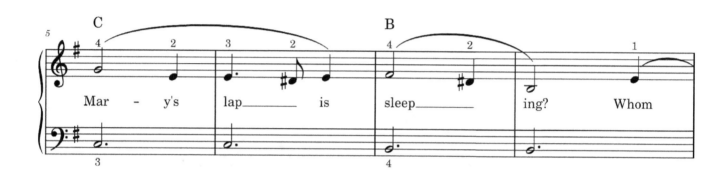
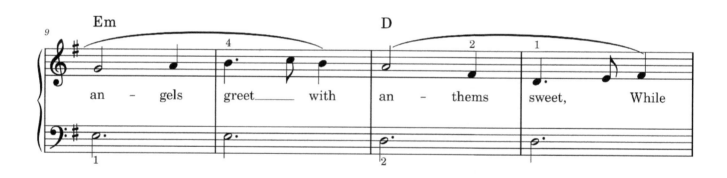
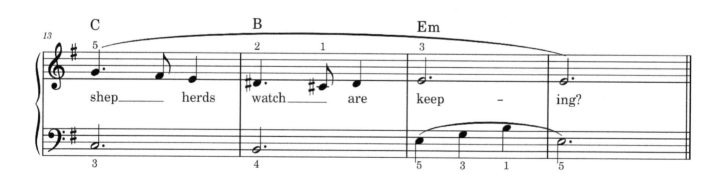

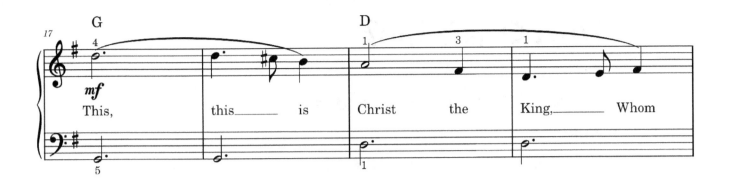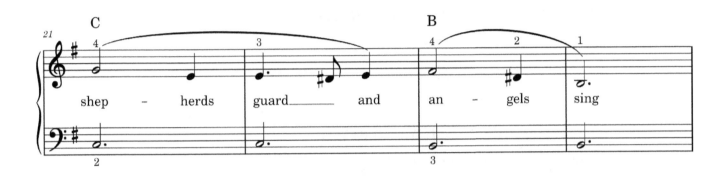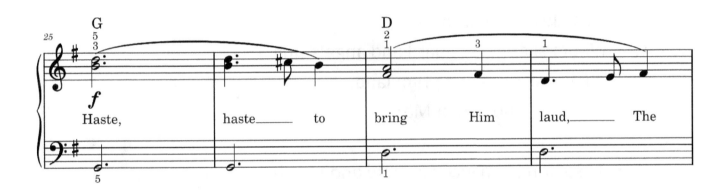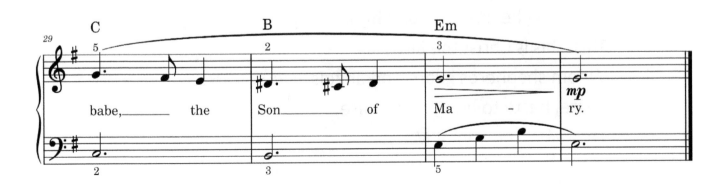

What Child is This?

1. What Child is this, who laid to rest,
On Mary's lap is sleeping?
Whom angels greet with anthems sweet,
While shepherds watch are keeping?
This, this is Christ the King,
Whom shepherds guard and angels sing
Haste, haste to bring Him laud,
The babe, the Son of Mary.

2. Why lies he in such mean estate
Where ox and ass are feeding,
The end of fear for all who hear
The silent Word is speaking.
This, this is Christ the King,
Whom shepherds guard and angels sing
Haste, haste to bring Him laud,
The babe, the Son of Mary.

3. So bring him incense, gold and myrrh
Come peasant king to love him;
The king of kings salvation brings
Let loving hearts enthrone him.
This, this is Christ the King,
Whom shepherds guard and angels sing
Haste, haste to bring Him praise,
The babe, the Son of Mary.

God Rest You Merry Gentlemen

God Rest You Merry Gentlemen

1. God rest you merry gentlemen
Let nothing you dismay
Remember Christ our Savior
Was born on Christmas Day
To save us all from Satan's pow'r
When we were gone astray
Oh tidings of comfort and joy
Comfort and joy
Oh tidings of comfort and joy

2. God rest ye merry gentlemen
Let nothing you dismay
Remember Christ our Savior
Was born on Christmas Day
To save us all from Satan's pow'r
When we were gone astray
Oh tidings of comfort and joy
Comfort and joy
Oh tidings of comfort and joy

3. In Bethlehem, in Israel
This blessed Babe was born
And laid within a manger
Upon this blessed morn
The which His Mother Mary
Did nothing take in scorn
Oh tidings of comfort and joy
Comfort and joy
Oh tidings of comfort and joy

Silent Night

Words: Joseph Mohr, 1792-1848
Music: Franz Gruber, 1787-1863

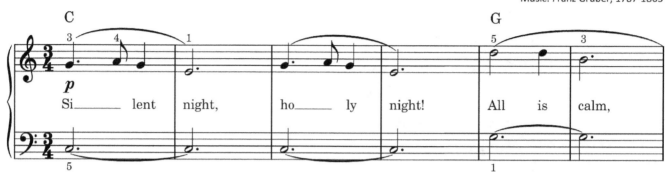
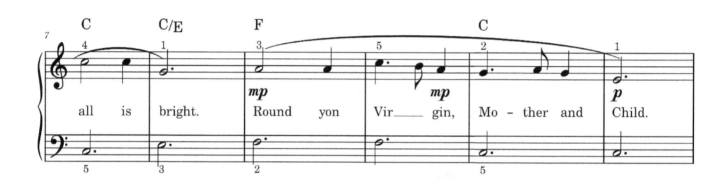
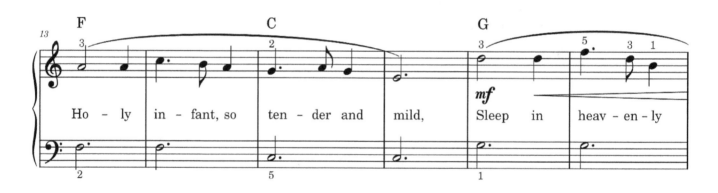
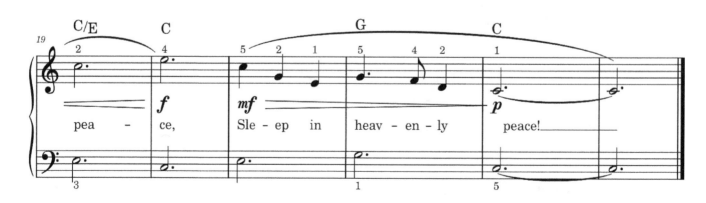

Silent Night

1. Silent night, holy night!
All is calm, all is bright.
Round yon Virgin, Mother and Child.
Holy infant so tender and mild,
Sleep in heavenly peace,
Sleep in heavenly peace!

2. Silent night, holy night!
Shepherds quake at the sight.
Glories stream from heaven afar.
Heavenly hosts sing Alleluia,
Christ the Saviour is born,
Christ the Saviour is born!

3. Silent night, holy night!
Son of God love's pure light.
Radiant beams from Thy holy face.
With dawn of redeeming grace,
Jesus Lord, at Thy birth.
Jesus Lord, at Thy birth!

O Christmas Tree

Words: Ernst Anschutz, ca. 1824
Music: Melchior Franck, ca. 16th Century

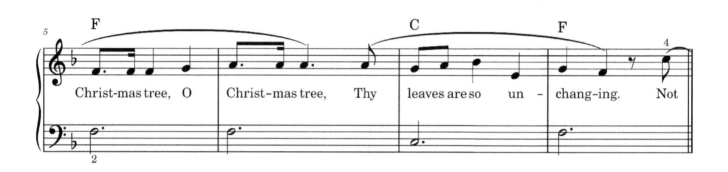
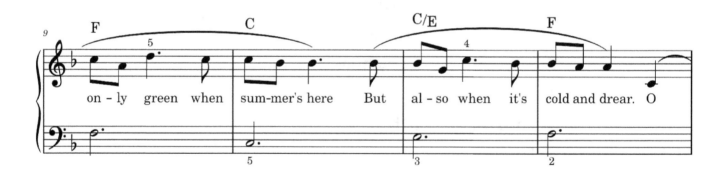
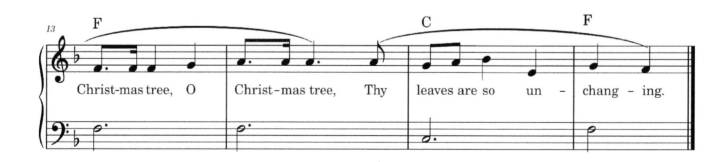

O Christmas Tree

1. O Christmas tree, o Christmas tree
Thy leaves are so unchanging.
O Christmas tree, o Christmas tree
Thy leaves are so unchanging.
Not only green when summer's here
But also when it's cold and drear.
O Christmas tree, o Christmas tree
Thy leaves are so unchanging.

2. O Christmas tree, o Christmas tree
Such pleasure do you bring me.
O Christmas tree, o Christmas tree
Such pleasure do you bring me.
For every year this Christmas tree
Brings to us such joy and glee.
O Christmas tree, o Christmas tree
Such pleasure do you bring me.

3. O Christmas tree, o Christmas tree
You'll ever be unchanging.
A symbol of goodwill and love
You'll ever be unchanging.
Each shining light, each silver bell
No one alive spreads cheer so well.
O Christmas tree, o Christmas tree
You'll ever be unchanging.

O Holy Night

Words: John Sullivan Dwight, 1813–1893
Music: Adolphe Charles Adam, 1803-1856

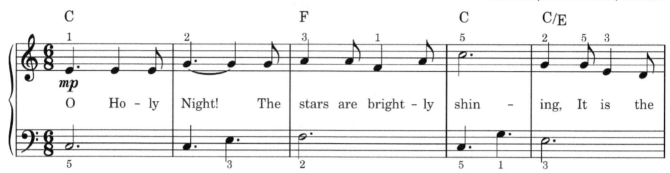
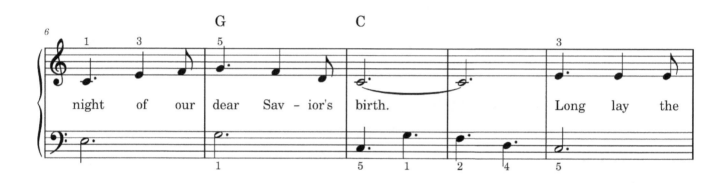
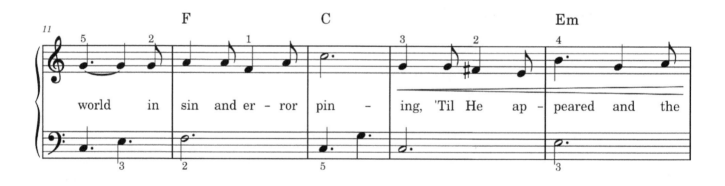
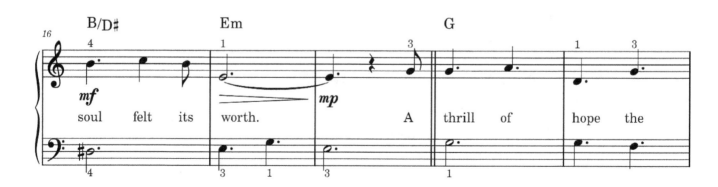

O Holy Night

1. O Holy Night! The stars are brightly shining
It is the night of our dear Savior's birth!
Long lay the world in sin and error pining,
'Till He appeared and the soul felt its worth.
A thrill of hope the weary world rejoices,
For yonder breaks a new and glorious morn!
Fall on your knees; Oh, hear the Angel voices!
O night divine, O night when Christ was born!
O night, O Holy night, O night divine!

2. Led by the light of Faith serenely beaming
With glowing hearts by His cradle we stand
So led by light of a star sweetly gleaming
Here come the Wise Men from Orient land
The King of kings lay thus in lowly manger
In all our trials born to be our friend
He knows our need, to our weakness is no stranger
Behold your King; before Him lowly bend
Behold your King; before Him lowly bend.

3. Truly He taught us to love one another;
His law is love and His Gospel is Peace
Chains shall He break, for the slave is our brother
And in His name, all oppression shall cease
Sweet hymns of joy in grateful chorus raise we
Let all within us Praise His Holy name
Christ is the Lord; O praise His name forever!
His power and glory evermore proclaim
His power and glory evermore proclaim.

Ding Dong Merrily on High

Words: George'a Ratcliffea Woodwarda, 1848–1934
Music: Jehan Tabourot, 1519-1593

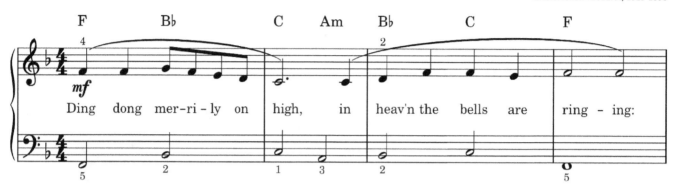
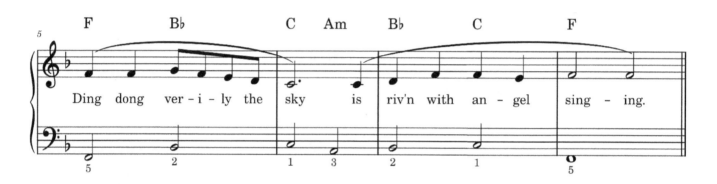
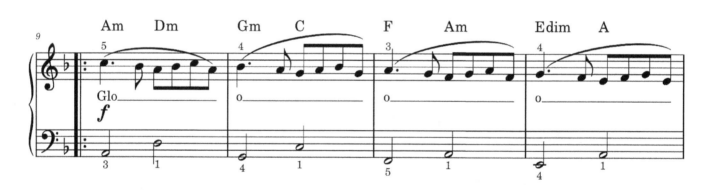
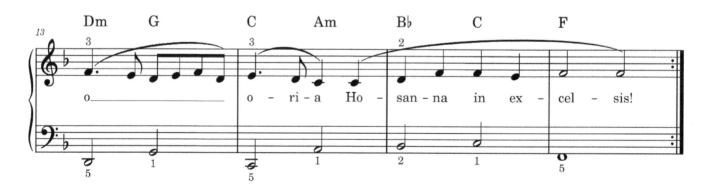

Ding Dong Merrily on High

1. Ding dong merrily on high,
In heav'n the bells are ringing:
Ding dong verily the sky
Is riv'n with angel singing.
>Gloria... Hosanna in excelsis!
>Gloria... Hosanna in excelsis!

2. E'en so here below, below,
Let steeple bells be swungen,
And "Io, io, io!"
By priest and people sungen.
>Gloria... Hosanna in excelsis!
>Gloria... Hosanna in excelsis!

3. Pray you, dutifully prime
Your matin chime, ye ringers;
May you beautifully rhyme
Your evetime song, ye singers.
>Gloria... Hosanna in excelsis!
>Gloria... Hosanna in excelsis!

O Come, All Ye Faithful
Adeste Fideles

Words: John F. Wade, ca. 1711-1786
Music: John F. Wade, ca. 1711-1786

O Come, All Ye Faithful

1. O come, all ye faithful, joyful and triumphant!
O come ye, O come ye, to Bethlehem.
Come and behold Him,
Born the King of Angels.
O come, let us adore Him,
O come, let us adore Him,
O come, let us adore Him,
Christ the Lord!

2. God of God, Light of Light.
Lo, He abhors not the Virgin's womb
Very God
Begotten, not created.
O come, let us adore Him,
O come, let us adore Him,
O come, let us adore Him,
Christ the Lord!

3. Sing, choirs of angels, sing in exultation
Sing, all ye citizens of heaven above!
Glory to God
All glory in the highest.
O come, let us adore Him,
O come, let us adore Him,
O come, let us adore Him,
Christ the Lord!

Hark! the Herald Angels Sing

Hark! the Herald Angels Sing

1. Hark! the Herald angels sing:
"Glory to the newborn King!"
Peace on earth and mercy mild
God and sinners reconciled.
Joyful, all ye nations rise
Join the triumph of the skies.
With angelic host proclaim:
"Christ is born in Bethlehem"
Hark! the Herald angels sing:
"Glory to the newborn King!"

2. Christ by highest Heav'n adored
Christ the everlasting Lord!
Late in time behold Him come
Offspring of a Virgin's womb
Veiled in flesh the Godhead see;
Hail the incarnate Deity
Pleased as man with man to dwell
Jesus, our Emmanuel
Hark! the herald angels sing:
"Glory to the newborn King!"

3. Hail the Heav'n-born Prince of Peace!
Hail the Son of Righteousness!
Light and life to all He brings
Ris'n with healing in His wings
Mild He lays His glory by
Born that man no more may die
Born to raise the sons of earth
Born to give them second birth
Hark! the herald angels sing:
"Glory to the newborn King!"

Away in a Manger

Words: Anon., ca. 1882, Philadelphia
Music: "Cradle Song" by William J. Kirkpatrick

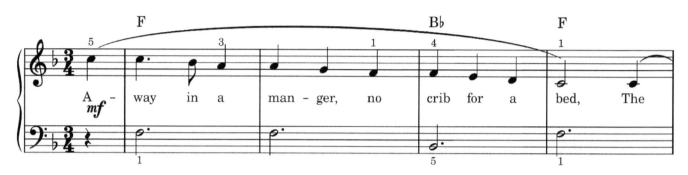
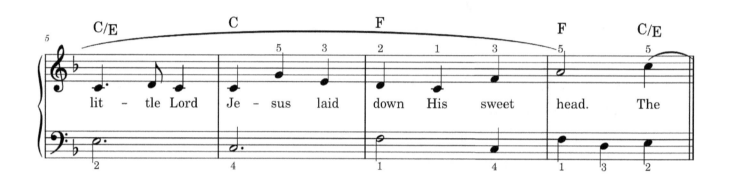
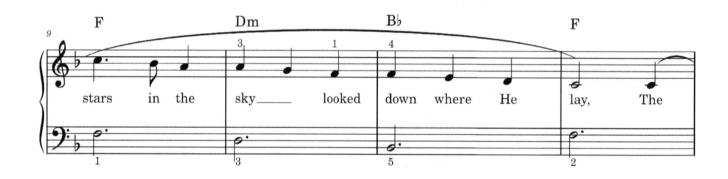
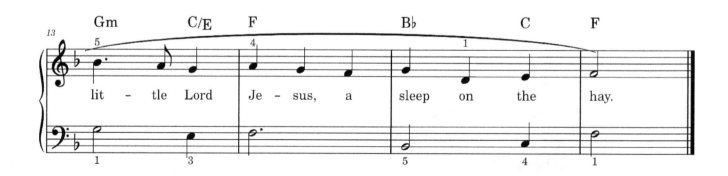

Away in a Manger

1. Away in a manger, no crib for a bed,
   The little Lord Jesus laid down His sweet head;
   The stars in the sky looked down where He lay,
   The little Lord Jesus, a sleep on the hay.

2. The cattle are lowing, the Baby awakes,
   But little Lord Jesus, no crying He makes;
   I love Thee, Lord Jesus, look down from the sky,
   And stay by my cradle till morning is nigh.

3. Be near me, Lord Jesus, I ask Thee to stay
   Close by me forever, and love me, I pray;
   Bless all the dear children in Thy tender care,
   And fit us for Heaven to live with Thee there.

The First Noel

Words: Cornish. Edited by William Sandys, ca. 1823
Music: Traditional English Carol

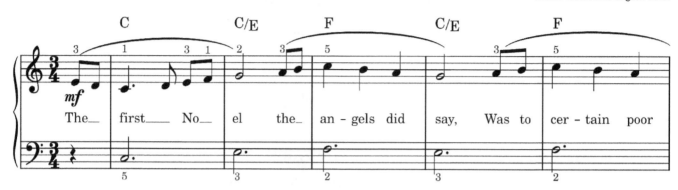
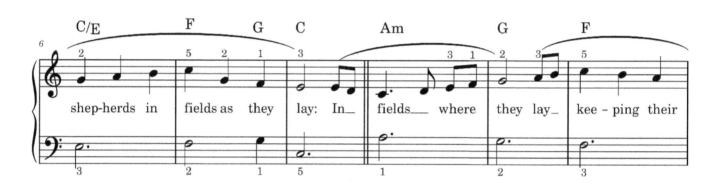

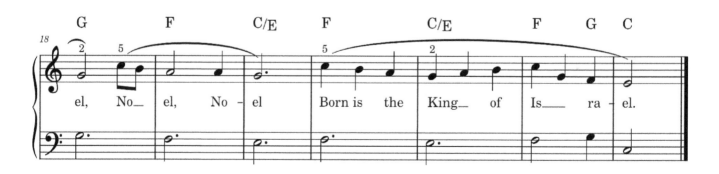

The First Noel

1. The first Noel the angels did say,
    Was to certain poor shepherds in fields as they lay:
    In fields where they lay keeping their sheep,
    On a cold winter's night that was so deep.
        Noel, Noel, Noel, Noel
        Born is the King of Israel.

2. They looked up and saw a star
    Shining in the east beyond them far
    And to the earth it gave great light
    And so it continued both day and night.
        Noel, Noel, Noel, Noel
        Born is the King of Israel.

3. And by the light of that same star
    Three Wise men came from country far
    To seek for a King was their intent
    And to follow the star wherever it went.
        Noel, Noel, Noel, Noel
        Born is the King of Israel.

4. This star drew nigh to the northwest
    O'er Bethlehem it took its rest
    And there it did both stop and stay
    Right o'er the place where Jesus lay.
        Noel, Noel, Noel, Noel
        Born is the King of Israel.

Up on the Housetop

Words: Benjamin Hanby, ca. 1864
Music: Benjamin Hanby, ca. 1864

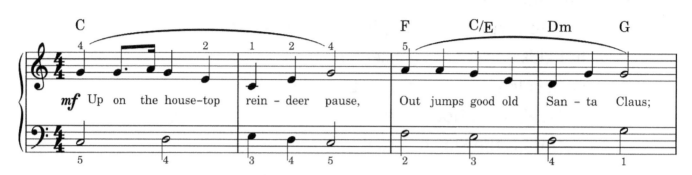
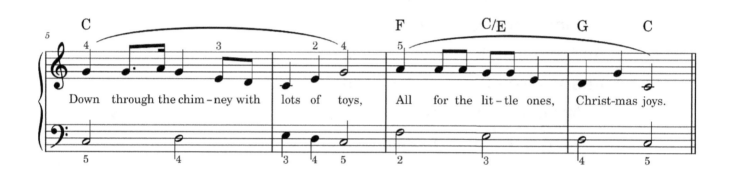
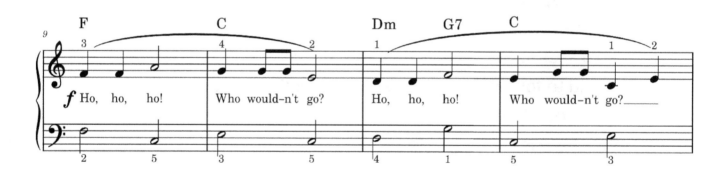
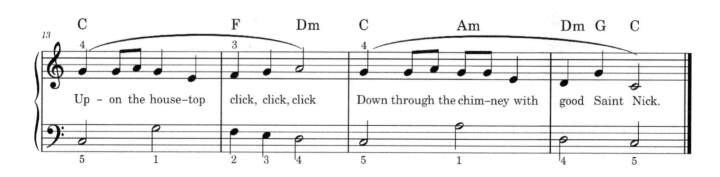

Up on the Housetop

1. Up on the housetop
Reindeer pause,
Out jumps good old Santa Claus;
Down through the chimney
With lots of toys,
All for the little ones,
Christmas joys
    Ho, ho, ho!
    Who wouldn't go?
    Ho, ho, ho!
    Who wouldn't go
    Up on the housetop
    Click, click, click
    Down through the chimney
    With good Saint Nick.

2. First comes the stocking
Of little Nell
Oh, dear Santa fill it well
Give her a dolly that
Laughs and cries
One that will open and
Shut her eyes
    Ho, ho, ho!

3. Next comes the
Stocking of little Will
Oh just see what a glorious fill
Here is a hammer and lots of tacks
Also a ball and a whip that cracks
    Ho, ho, ho!

Angels We Have Heard On High

Words: James Montgomery, 1771-1854
Music: Henry Smart, 1867; tune of "Regent Square"

Angels We Have Heard on High

1. Angels we have heard on high
Sweetly singing o'er the plains,
And the mountains in reply
Echoing their joyous strains.
Gloria, in excelsis Deo.
Gloria, in excelsis Deo.

2. Angels we have heard on high
Sweetly, sweetly through the night
And the mountains in reply
Echoing their brief delight.
Gloria, in excelsis Deo...

3. Shepherds, why this jubilee?
Why your joyous strains prolong?
What the gladsome tidings be
Which inspire your heavenly song?
Gloria, in excelsis Deo...

4. Come to Bethlehem and see
Him whose birth the angels sing,
Come, adore on bended knee,
Christ the Lord, the newborn King.
Gloria, in excelsis Deo...

Joy to the World

Words: Isaac Watts, 1674-1748
Music: George F. Handel, 1685-1759

Joy to the World

1. Joy to the world! The Lord is come;
Let earth receive her King!
Let every heart prepare Him room,
And heaven and nature sing,
And heaven and nature sing,
And heaven, and heaven, and nature sing.

2. Joy to the world! the Saviour reigns;
Let men their songs employ;
While fields and floods, rocks, hills, and plains
Repeat the sounding joy,
Repeat the sounding joy,
Repeat, repeat the sounding joy.

3. No more let sins and sorrows grow,
Nor thorns infest the ground;
He comes to make His blessings flow
Far as the curse is found,
Far as the curse is found,
Far as, far as, the curse is found.

4. He rules the world with truth and grace,
And makes the nations prove
The glories of His righteousness,
And wonders of His love,
And wonders of His love,
And wonders, wonders, of His love.

Deck the Halls

Words: Thomas Oliphant, ca. 1862
Music: Welsh Traditional, ca. 16th Century

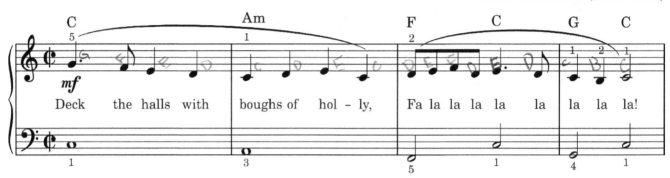
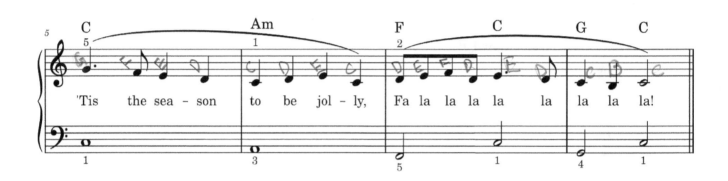
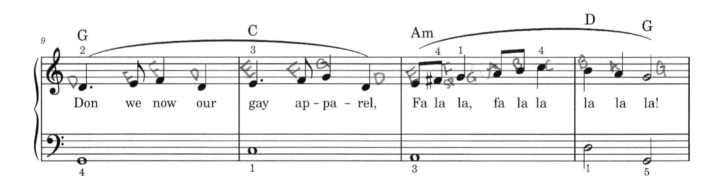
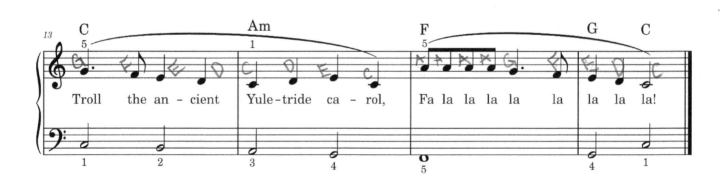

Deck the Halls

1. Deck the halls with boughs of holly,
Fa, la, la, la, la, la, la, la, la!
'Tis the season to be jolly,
Fa, la, la, la, la, la, la, la, la!
Don we now our gay apparel
Fa, la, la, la, la, la, la, la!
Troll the ancient Yule-tride carol,
Fa, la, la, la, la, la, la, la, la!

2. See the blazing Yule before us,
Fa, la, la, la, la, la, la, la, la!
Strike the harp and join the chorus.
Fa, la, la, la, la, la, la, la, la!
Follow me in merry measure,
Fa, la, la, la, la, la, la, la!
While I tell of Yule-tride treasure,
Fa, la, la, la, la, la, la, la, la!

3. Fast away the old year passes,
Fa, la, la, la, la, la, la, la, la!
Hail the new, ye lads and lasses!
Fa, la, la, la, la, la, la, la, la!
Sing we joyous all together
Fa, la, la, la, la, la, la, la!
Heedless of the wind and weather,
Fa, la, la, la, la, la, la, la, la!

Carol of the Bells

Mykola Dmytrovych Leontovych, 1877–1921

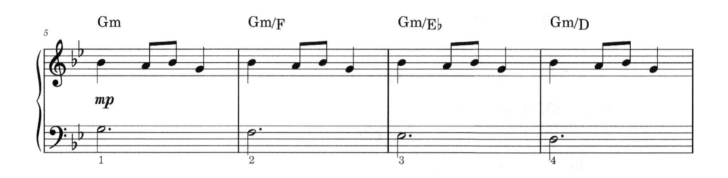
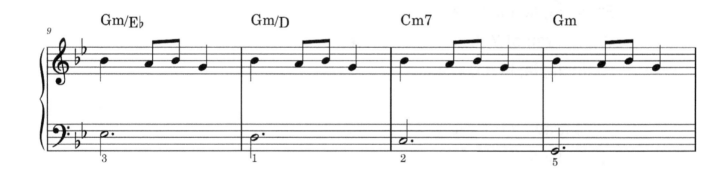

Note Names on Keyboard and Staff

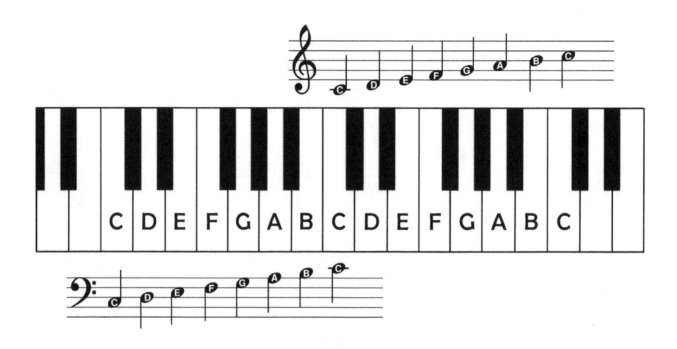

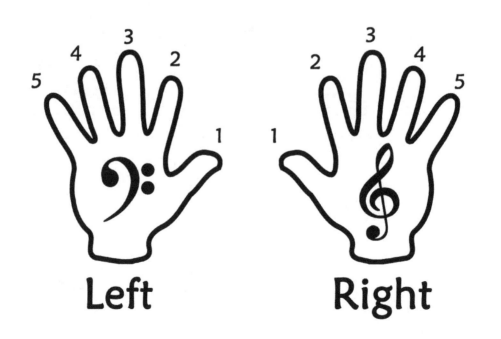

Left   Right

Notes and Rest

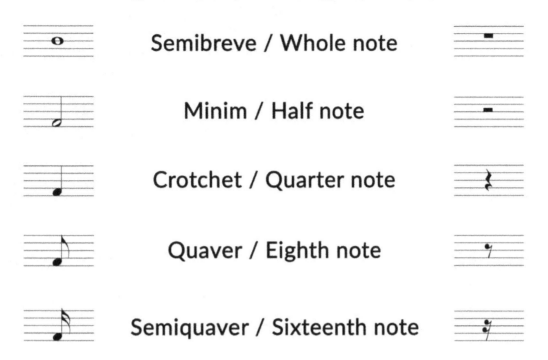

Rhythm Tree

Length gets reduced by half for each step in the tree

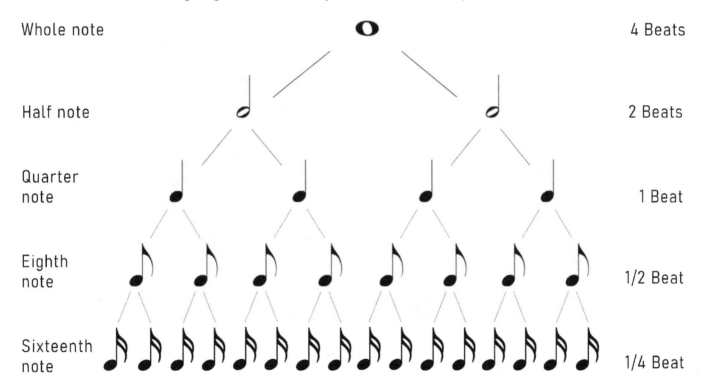

Piano Chords 1

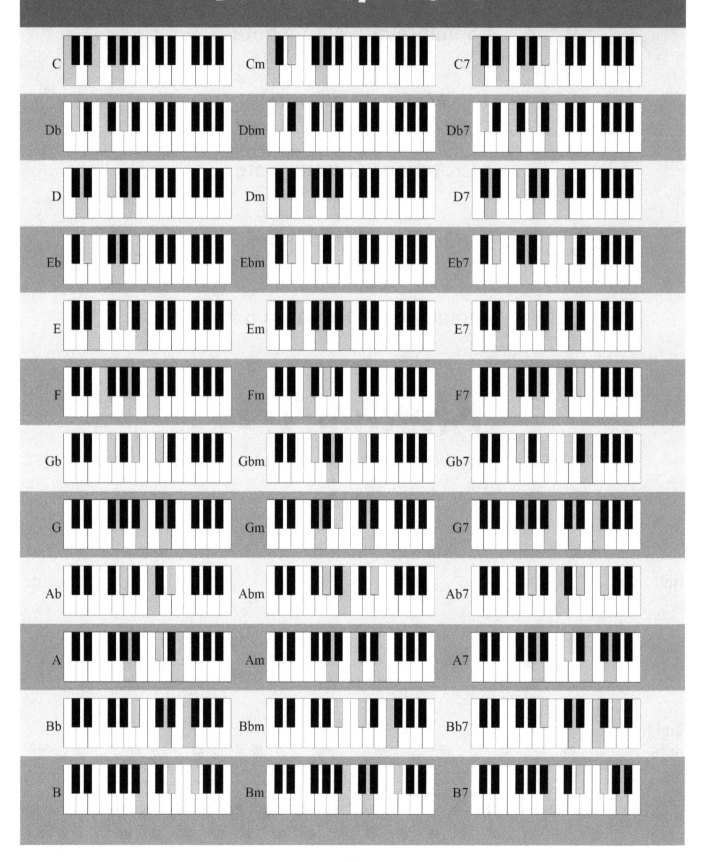

Piano Chords 2

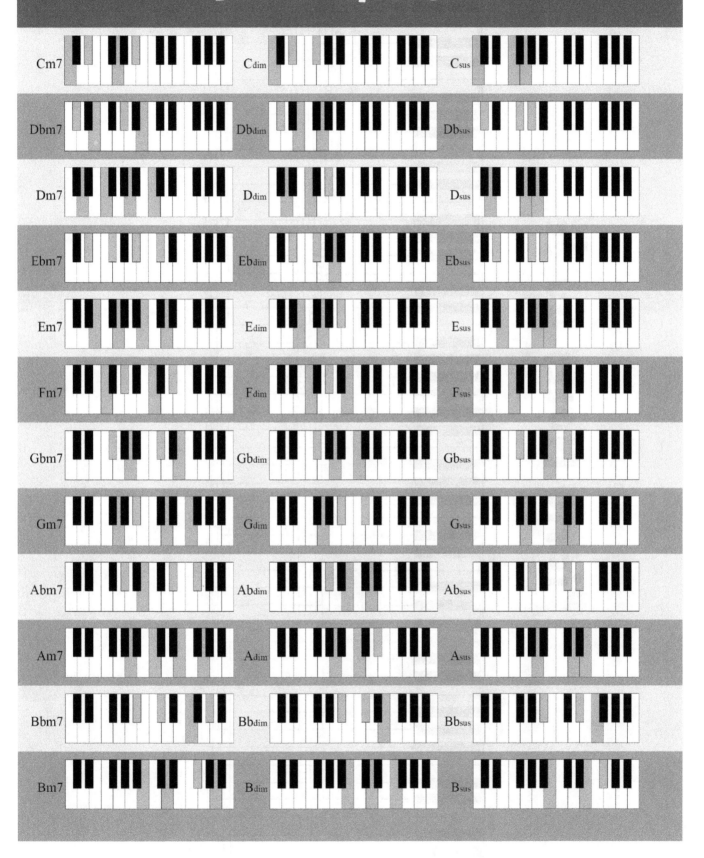

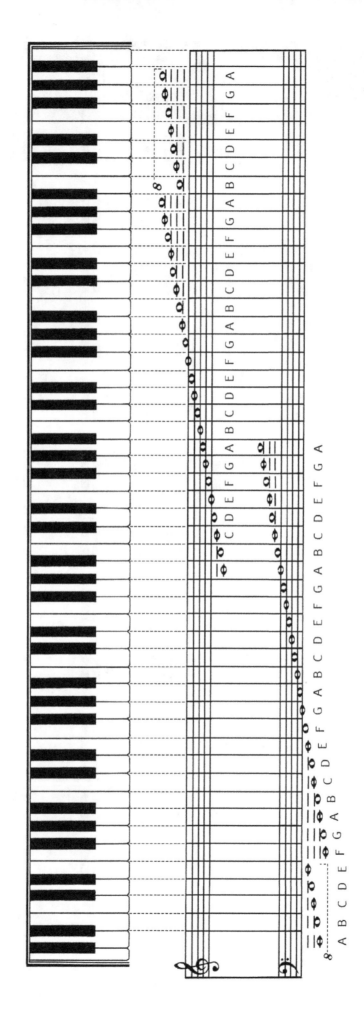

Circle of Fifths

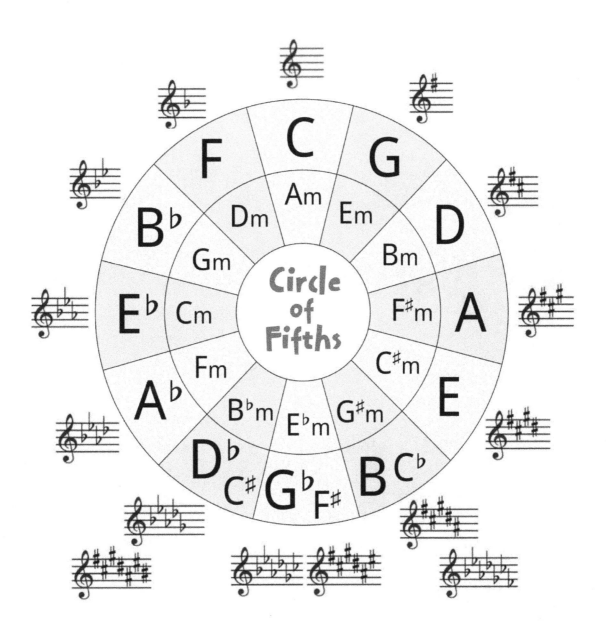

Are you enjoying this awesome book?

If so, **please leave me a review.**

I'm very interested in your feedback to create even better products for you to enjoy shortly.

Visit my webside at:

www.youtube.com/EasyPianoMusic

or scan the QR code below to see

all of my creative products!

Thank you very much!

Alicja Urbanowicz

SEE OTHER ARRANGEMENTS FOR PIANO

  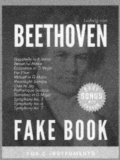  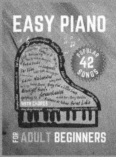

    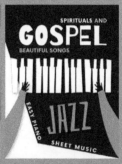

YouTube.com/EasyPianoMusic

CPSIA information can be obtained
at www.ICGtesting.com
Printed in the USA
BVHW021717051222
653487BV00012B/703